Managing God's Money: The Basics

Workbook

Michel A. Bell, F.C.C.A, S.M.

Managing God's Money—The Basics Workbook
Copyright © 2001, Michel A. Bell

ISBN: 1-55306-197-7

Essence Publishing is a Christian Book Publisher dedicated to furthering the work of Christ through the written word. For more information, contact: 44 Moira Street West, Belleville, Ontario, Canada K8P 1S3. Phone: 1-800-238-6376 • Fax: (613) 962-3055. E-mail: info@essencegroup.com • Internet: www.essencegroup.com

Essence
PUBLISHING

Belleville, Ontario, Canada

To:

Doreen
Bill & Keisha
Adrienne, Jesse & Dylan
Shabbir & Lesley Ann

Twins!

Essential Concepts

The GAS Principle: Three Key Truths in the Bible concerning money:
- **Key Truth #1: God Owns Everything** (Psalm 24:1, Colossians 1:16).
- **Key Truth #2: Accept What You Have** (1 Timothy 6:7-8, Hebrews 13:5).
- **Key Truth #3: Seek First His Kingdom and Submit Your Requests to Him** (Matthew 6:33, Proverbs 19:21).

The PEACE Budgetary Control System: A system that allows you to achieve **goals** systematically in the following manner:
- **P**lan for a specific period to accomplish precise **goals**.
- **E**stimate and record the expenses needed to achieve those **goals**.
- **A**ct on the **plan and record** actual results as you progress towards your **goals**.
- **C**ompare actual results **with** the **plan** and with the **estimated expenses** required to attain the **goals**.
- **E**xecute changes necessary to remain on course to realize the **goals**.

The PLANE Spending Analysis: Five questions to answer before you commit to any major expenditure:
- **P** Did I **plan** this expenditure and did I include it in my budget?
- **L** Will the expenditure increase my **loans**?
- **A** Are there realistic **alternatives** to achieve my spending objective?
- **N** Is the expenditure **necessary** to achieve my spending objective?
- **E** Is this the most **effective** use of resources now, relative to my **life goals and budget goals**?

A goal is your **destination**: where you wish to go.
- **A plan** is your **journey**: the steps to achieve your **goal**.
  - **An estimate** is the likely cost of the **plan**: the cost of the steps in the **plan**.
    - **A budget** is a record of the results of the **planning** and **estimating** processes.

Contents

Acknowledgements

Once again I am indebted to my children! Lesley Ann, thanks for writing the foreword, reviewing most of the workbook, and for your infectious excitement! Bill, Keisha, and Shabbir, thanks for your continuing inspiration.

Dave Smith, senior pastor of Fairview Alliance Church, Dollard Des Ormeaux, Quebec, and Greg Hazle, thanks for your comments on several chapters of this workbook.

My dear wife, Doreen, this poem, "My Wife, My Friend," that I wrote on our 26th wedding anniversary conveys precisely my words of thanks to you for your prayers and support on this project. The passage of time merely reinforces the message.

My Wife, My Friend

Another year has passed
and your wisdom you continue to impart,
my wife, my friend.
Your deep friendship I treasure
the more your wise counsel I receive,
my wife, my friend.
As you celebrate this special day
I want to say thanks for keeping His light aglow.
Truly you are special to so many searching souls
as His message shines forth through your walk.
I know I am blessed with you by my side
my counsellor, my lover, my wife, my friend,
I thank God that He chose you to stand beside me,
dressed in His armour prepared for His triumphant return.
My darling, my friend, my dedicated wife,
thank you for your devotion, your unselfish love and support.
Truly I love you now and forever more.

© Michel A. Bell, March 1996

To God be the Glory!

Foreword

In a time when debt and day trading are common household occurrences, one needs to ask, what really matters? Forget the fluff, go to the core, what is the real issue? In this book, Mike touches on the treasure, the meat, and the true heart of the issue—Money and the Cross. An oxymoron to most—yet an issue that most of us do not understand or even want to begin exploring. However, he meshes these two together and brings clarity to God's teachings on stewardship and managing God's money. It does not have to be a never-ending rat race, in which one feels swallowed up by debt and consumed by money. Let God set you free!

As I read the draft of this workbook, Mike's heart was visible! His passion for Jesus and evangelism, and his dream for everyone to be financially free in Christ shone through. He takes us step by step, teaching us how to take control of our personal financial situation by learning, understanding, and implementing God's teachings. This book simply goes farther than your average budget planner; it lets you glean for yourself God's view on money and His plan for your life.

We all stumble, and we all fall financially. However, we have to get up, dust ourselves off, and learn from our mistakes. Do we really understand God's view on money? This book goes a long way to help us understand God's money management strategies and to show us how managing His money really works. Take a leap of faith, and let God set you free—He is capable of anything.

Ah, Lord GOD! Behold, You have made the heavens and the earth by Your great power and outstretched arm. There is nothing too hard for You (Jeremiah 32:17 NKJV).

Lesley Ann Bell
Langley, British Columbia

Introduction

If you are like me, generally, you do not read instruction manuals. They are boring! Instead, you try to figure things out as you go. Why not? It's a challenge! Isn't it? I dare not say it's more fun! Oftentimes, we get the equipment we bought to function without reading the manual—although mainly sub-optimally—only after several frustrating hours of tinkering!

Many of us take the same approach to life! We go through life without reading and understanding the instruction manual that was prepared especially for us—the Bible! We try to figure things out on our own. We engage in endless debates over issues about which the Bible gives clear guidance, such as money and possessions.

Yes, folks, the Bible is the instruction manual for life. It has everything we **need** to know about life, today, and tomorrow. Yet it is amazing how little time we spend studying it! Let me share two quotations from Noah Webster, statesman, educator, and author of Webster's Dictionary; he said: "God's Word, contained in the Bible, has furnished all necessary rules to direct our conduct..." and "...education is useless without the Bible."[1]

Noah Webster made these profound statements in the early 19th century, and although there is much opposition to them today, still they are relevant.

Many of us have money problems: we get into debt; we spend consistently more than we earn; and we try to increase our debt as one way out! In my experience, most of these money problems are symptomatic of attitudinal problems—the remedies of which are in the Bible. Most important, however, we do not appreciate that in the Bible there is comfort for those suffering from these problems.

Jesus Christ is the perfect Father, who has given those who surrender their lives to Him several assurances, including John 16:24 (NRSV): "Until now you have not asked for anything in my name. Ask and you will receive, so that your joy may be complete." When our circumstances seem difficult and indeed are difficult, Jesus can solve these problems in His time! Unfortunately, we do not always think about relying on Jesus for our daily sustenance and encouragement. Therefore, we are not able to encounter Him regularly to receive His blessings!

We must get to know and understand what the Bible teaches so that we can do what it says. Even more important, however, we must get to know as our personal Lord and Saviour, the ultimate author of the Bible: Jesus Christ. If you do not know Christ as your personal Lord and Saviour, I urge you to make that commitment today. Today is "your present." Open it, use it, and experience it, because you may not receive another tomorrow!

This workbook complements my book, *Managing God's Money—The Basics.*[2] You may use it alone, but you will not get the full benefits. In it, I have tried to include a collection of Bible verses that deal with the key factors I propound in *Managing God's Money—The Basics*. The questions shown throughout require thoughtful reflection and will unearth additional truths. I believe that both individuals and groups will find this workbook helpful as they see **biblical examples about goal-setting, planning, prayer, giving,** and much more.

I pray that you will be blessed as you work through this book.

---

[1] William J. Federer, *America's God And Country*, (Coppell, TX FAME Publishing Inc., 1994) p. 676.

[2] Michel A. Bell, *Managing God's Money*, (Belleville, Ontario, Essence Publishing, 2000).

1

All Scripture is God-breathed and is useful for teaching,
rebuking, correcting and training in righteousness
(2 Timothy 3:16 NIV).

Money and Three Key Truths

Money and Three Key Truths

Money must be important to God. The Bible devotes twice as many verses to money than to faith and prayer combined. Jesus said more about money than about heaven and hell! Fifteen percent of Jesus' recorded words were about money. He said more about money and possessions than any other single thing! [1] Money and possessions are important to God!

So what is money? It is the means of exchange that replaced the barter system, centuries ago, under which goods of equivalent value were traded—oil for wool and so on. Money is the instrument we use to pay for things we buy: cash, cheques, credit cards, debit cards, loans from banks, private sources, merchants and other means that give us access to goods and services.

Soon money will be invisible, which is quite scary because controlling our spending will become more difficult! This so called **electronic money** (primarily **"smart cards"**) will function like today's credit and debit cards! Already we have the perfect vehicle for spending electronic money: the Internet! Having become the shopping location of choice for many, the Internet will contribute to the continued increase of credit card debt.

What are the consequences of this? Unless we understand our role concerning money and possessions and learn to manage and control our time, our spending, and other resources, these things will control us!

Therefore, we must learn the many truths in the Bible about money, possessions, and other resources—primarily the Three Key Truths. Will we become rich once we get to know, understand, and implement them? I don't know... maybe. This is a complex question. What is rich?

- Was Mother Teresa rich in the abject poverty in which she lived in Calcutta? My wife and I visited Calcutta and saw the poverty in which she ministered; we believe she was a "rich" woman!

- Were the Apostles, who followed Jesus without material possessions, rich? Walking with Jesus as they did must have been an incredibly rich experience!

Jesus has told us to come to Him and He will give us rest, to cast our burdens on Him, to knock, to seek, to ask, and He will respond.... In Him, I submit, we will find **riches**! Not in money!

10. **Explain Ecclesiastes 2:26.**

_____
_____
_____
_____

11. **Rewrite Proverbs 13:7 in your own words.**

_____
_____
_____
_____

The foundation of this money management system is Three Key Truths from the Bible which collectively I call the GAS principle:

Key Truth #1: God Owns Everything.

Key Truth #2: Accept What You Have.

Key Truth #3: Seek First His Kingdom and Submit Your Requests to Him.

12. Read Psalm 24:1-2 and Colossians 1:16-17 and respond as requested below:
12.1 Write one sentence that expresses the message in these verses.

_____

_____

_____

_____

12.2 Since God owns everything, how should we approach money management (Luke 12:42-48)?

_____

_____

_____

_____

13. Read 1 Timothy 6:6-10 and Hebrews 13:5 and reply as requested:
13.1 Write one sentence that expresses the message in these verses.

_____

_____

_____

_____

13.2 What do you understand by the statement "being content with what you have"?

_____

_____

_____

_____

14. Read Matthew 6:24-33 and respond to the questions below:
14.1 Identify at least three promises from Jesus that you will start to follow today. Rewrite these promises in your own words.

_____

_____

_____

_____

14.2 According to verses 25 and 26, why should you not worry about your life?

_____

_____

_____

_____

14.3 Comment on the similarities between verses 25 and 26 and Romans 8:32.

_____

_____

_____

_____

15. **Read Proverbs 19:21 and indicate how it should impact our plans.**

_____

_____

_____

_____

16. **Do you believe the Three Key Truths? If you answer other than an unqualified "yes," please explain.**

_____

_____

_____

_____

17. **Since God owns everything, we own nothing! Not the house, nor the car, nor the watch! Do you agree? Yes or no?**

_____

_____

_____

_____

18. **Do the Key Truths apply to your life, your time, your talents, "your" money, "your" possessions, and your family? Explain.**

_____

_____

_____

_____

19. **Since God owns everything, we are His managers or stewards. What is the role of a steward?**

_____

_____

_____

_____

20. **Read Matthew 25:14-30 and answer the following questions:**

20.1 With which of the three servants do you identify most readily? Why?

_____

_____

_____

_____

My Stewardship Covenant With Jesus[2]

Jesus Christ has given me specific abilities and talents. He has given me all the time that I need, all the resources that I need, and the family that I have. He will give me everything that I need in the future, when I need it.

He is my Lord and my Saviour. I acknowledge that I am responsible to Him for the way I live my life; for full utilization of my talents and abilities; for full utilization of the time He gives me; and for every possession that He entrusts to me, all for His glory.

Every minute of each day, and in all things that I do, I promise to bring Him glory. I know that all this I am able to do by His grace. I am confident that one day I will stand face to face with Him to give an account of my stewardship.

Finally, I acknowledge that I am accountable to my brothers and sisters in Christ to discharge this responsibility daily.

Signed:_____ Witness:_____

Date: _____

20.2 Does the parable imply that the onus is on us to determine the abilities that we have and to use them for God's glory? Explain.

_____

_____

_____

_____

20.3 Based on your understanding of this parable, define "stewardship" and "steward."

_____

_____

_____

_____

20.4 Would you enter into the stewardship covenant on the previous page? Explain.

_____

_____

_____

_____

20.5 Do you agree that you have enough time, the necessary abilities, and all the resources necessary to do the things God called you to do? Explain.

_____

_____

_____

_____

20.6 Are you making optimum use of God's resources for His glory? Explain.

_____

_____

_____

_____

---

[1] Randy Alcorn, Money Wealth and Possessions (Wheaton, Illinois: Tyndale House Publishers, Inc. 1989), pp. 16-17.

[2] A married man would add the following, "I acknowledge that I am His representative as head of my family in the home that He has provided, where I promise always to be an example of His love, ready to lay down my life for my wife."

Personal Notes

2

I am the good shepherd. The good shepherd
lays down his life for the sheep.

(John 10:11 NIV).

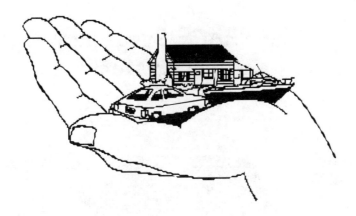

Critical Money Management Step #1
Establishing Where You Are
with the Shepherd

* * *

Your "Eternal Worth"

Three Critical Money Management Steps

Managing God's money effectively includes embracing the **PEACE** Budgetary Control System,[1] applying the **GAS** principle, and **PLANE** spending analysis[2] to all spending decisions. First, however, you must complete **three critical steps**:

1 Establish where you are with the Shepherd—your **eternal worth**.

2 Establish where you are with His resources—your **material worth**.

3 Establish long and short-term goals—your **destination**.

The PEACE Budgetary Control System

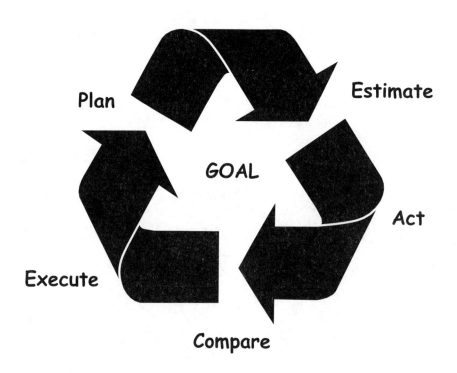

Plan

Estimate

GOAL

Act

Execute

Compare

Critical Money Management Step #1

(Establish where you are with the Shepherd—your "Eternal Worth")

Over the years, as Chief Financial Officer of several subsidiaries of Alcan, I have had to know and implement the company's principles, policies and practices. I could not be successful otherwise. Similarly, to manage God's money effectively, you must know Him and His Word. Become Jesus' Chief Financial Officer now! Then you will spend His money based on the principles in the Bible. Follow the **Good Shepherd!**

21. **Read John 10:27-30 and respond to the following questions:**
21.1 Who is the Good Shepherd?

_____

_____

_____

_____

21.2 Who are the sheep?

_____

_____

_____

_____

21.3 Can the sheep be lost? Explain.

_____

_____

_____

_____

22. **Read John 3:1-17 and answer these questions:**
22.1 Who was Nicodemus?

_____

_____

_____

_____

22.2 What does Jesus tell us about being born again (John 3:3-6)?

_____

_____

_____

_____

23. **Read Romans 3:23-26 and 6:23. Rewrite these verses in your own words.**

_____

_____

_____

_____

_____

_____

_____

_____

24. **Explain Romans 5:8.**

_____

_____

_____

_____

25. **What does Jesus say about Eternal Life in John 5:24?**

_____

_____

_____

26. **What does John the Baptist say about Eternal Life in John 3:36?**

_____

_____

_____

27. **What does Apostle John say about Eternal Life in 1 John 4:9?**

_____

_____

_____

_____

28. **What is "Eternal Life"?**

_____

_____

_____

_____

29. **Read Psalm 139:23-24 carefully.** Pray this prayer as David did. List any hindrances to a relationship with Christ that are revealed and ask the Lord to remove them.

_____

_____

_____

_____

_____

_____

_____

_____

30. **Where are you in Christ? Have you accepted Him as your Lord and Saviour?**

_____

_____

_____

_____

A Special Invitation from the Shepherd

Managing money is merely one aspect of life. It cannot be isolated from others. How we spend money helps to define who we are! Hence, I invite you to think about **a forever that you will remember**.

Jesus told the eminent Jewish teacher Nicodemus that he needed a spiritual rebirth to gain eternal life.[3] Likewise, He told His disciples, "...unless you change and become like children, you will never enter the kingdom of heaven."[4] I ask you to utilize the faith, sincerity, and humility that a child displays to her parents to accept Jesus' invitation for this **forever to remember**.

This will be your pivotal lifetime decision; it is easy, yet profound. As a prelude to deciding, acknowledge the following:

- Jesus Christ lived on earth, died, then rose from the dead.
- He is the only true and living God.
- The Bible is the Word of God (inspired) and is without error (infallible).
- You are a sinner, and you need to seek forgiveness.

Then from your heart, go for it!

- Decide to turn away from your sins (repent).
- Ask Jesus to forgive your sins.
- Ask Jesus to take control of your life (receive Jesus as Lord and Saviour).

When you accept Christ into your life, your world view changes as the Holy Spirit works within you. You may not become rich and famous, but you will gain direct access to our perfect Heavenly Father. Speak to Him! Listen to Him through His Word, the Bible! Start to attend a Bible-believing church! Meet with other Christians to encourage and to nurture you! Remember, His Word says He will never leave you or forsake you.[5]

31. **Read James 2:14-19 and 1 John 1:6. What is the common theme between them?**

_____

_____

_____

_____

---

[1] PEACE Budgetary Control System (Copyright © 1994-1999, Michel A. Bell).

[2] PLANE Spending Analysis (Copyright © 1997, Michel A. Bell).

[3] John 3:1-17.

[4] Matthew 18:3.

[5] Hebrews 13:5.

Personal Notes

3

To the man who pleases him, God gives wisdom, knowledge and happiness,
but to the sinner he gives the task of gathering and storing up wealth
to hand it over to the one who pleases God.
This too is meaningless, a chasing after the wind
(Ecclesiastes 2:26 NIV).

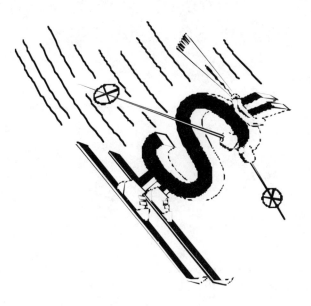

Critical Money Management Step #2
Establishing Where You Are
with God's Resources

* * *

Your "Material Worth"

(Establish where you are with God's resources—your "Material Worth")

Now you are ready to establish your Material Worth. You do this by preparing a net worth statement, which is a "still photograph" of your financial affairs at a specific date. It reflects what you "owned" (remember, God owns everything, so your ownership is in the form of a trustee-ship or stewardship) and what you owed at that date, and is the base from which you will travel during your money-management journey.

Here is an example of a net worth statement at 30 June 1999.

Net Worth ("Material Worth") Statement
As of 30 June 1999

Things I "Own" (Assets)	$
Cash	5,000
Personal Effects	15,000
Car	9,000
Furniture	20,000
House	150,000
Total	**199,000**
Things I "Owe" (Liabilities)	**$**
Family Loan	2,000
Other Loans	2,500
Car Loan	11,000
Credit Card	20,000
Mortgage	125,000
Total All Loans	**160,500**
Your Equity (Net Worth)	**38,500**
Total	**199,000**

We show amounts under "Own" at market value,[1] not at your cost to buy them; these are your assets. Notice the asset called "Personal Effects." Often we forget that we can sell some of these items. If you need cash urgently for a special expense that passes the various spending tests mentioned in chapter six, you may choose to sell one. Indeed, to reduce your debts, consider selling any other item under the "Own" heading that you do not require. However, do not take this decision lightly.

The total of each side of the statement is $199,000, but the "Equity" (which is total assets minus total liabilities) under the "Owe" heading is a mere $38,500 because you used loans (other people's money) to buy most of the assets! Items under "Owe" are your liabilities—amounts you owe.

The **Maximum Debt Ratio** is the total of all loans on the net worth statement as a percentage of total liabilities[2] [(160,500/199,000)*100]. The **Debt Repayment Ratio** is the total loan payments (including mortgage principal and interest) for the period (one year) as a percentage of gross income for the same period.[3]

32. **Compute the two ratios mentioned in the preceding paragraph for your situation.**

_____

_____

_____

_____

33. **Are you happy with the result in 32? Explain.**

_____

_____

_____

_____

34. **Which of the following factors would you consider in setting the target for the two ratios mentioned above: life goals, budget goals, your daughter's upcoming wedding (assume this applies), existing credit card balances? Comment on the potential impact of each factor on the ratios.**

_____

_____

_____

_____

_____

_____

_____

_____

35. **Currently, if these two ratios for you are high, what options do you have to reduce them in the short term?**

_____

_____

_____

_____

36. **Read Luke 12:15 and Colossians 3:5 and answer the following:**

36.1 Do you believe that "greed" is a factor that affects your spending habits? Yes or no.

_____

_____

_____

36.2 Review your spending (cheques, credit cards, debit charges, loans and others) over the past six months; then, answer the question in 36.1 again. Refer to the "Cash Flow" section below.

_____

_____

_____

_____

36.3 Are you happy with your spending pattern? Expand.

_____

_____

_____

_____

36.4 Did you identify any changes to your attitude towards money that you intend to implement as a result of the review in 36.2? List them here.

_____

_____

_____

_____

36.5 Write a brief statement of the changes you wish to make and the time frame for these changes. (When you get to the Life Goal section, transform this into **Goals**.)

_____

_____

_____

_____

Net Worth ("Material Worth") Statement

As At _____ (date)

Things I "Own" (Assets) $

Cash _____

Investments _____

Personal Effects _____

Car _____

Furniture _____

House _____

Others _____

Total

Things I "Owe" (Liabilities) $

Family Loans _____

Car Loan _____

Credit Card Balance _____

Mortgage _____

Others _____

Total All Loans

My Equity (Net Worth) Total _____

Analysis of Amounts Owing to Lenders

Lender's Name	$ Owing	Interest %	Comments

Borrowing

The Bible does not prohibit borrowing. Many Christians use Romans 13:8 to substantiate this point; it does not! The Bible states that you should not charge interest to the poor, and if you borrow, you must repay. Still, however, as God owns everything, you should strive to be debt free.[4]

37. **Explain Exodus 22:25-27 in your own words.**

_____

_____

_____

_____

38. **Explain Psalm 37:21 in your own words.**

_____

_____

_____

_____

39. **Rewrite Romans 13:8 in your own words.**

_____

_____

_____

_____

40. **Rewrite Proverbs 22:7-8 in your own words.**

_____

_____

_____

_____

41. **Explain Matthew 5:42.**

_____

_____

_____

_____

42. **Review your comments in 37-41 above. Do you agree that you should strive to be debt free? Please explain your answer.**

_____

_____

_____

_____

Cash Flows

Earlier we saw a net worth statement, which I described as a "still photograph" of what you owned (assets) and what you owed (liabilities). Obviously, it changes when you receive income, pay expenses, repay debts, or buy or sell assets. To capture these changes we need a "video camera" that we call a "cash flow" statement.

We divide this statement into two segments—Inflows and Outflows, as in the table below. **Inflows**, as the name implies, show **cash received**. **Outflows** reflect **cash paid**.

You have all the facts to prepare this statement! No consultant will have this information. Initially, the idea of you preparing a cash flow statement will seem daunting to you! However, the mystique goes when you realise that it shows merely the timing of funds you plan to get and to spend, and the net balance.

What conclusions can we draw from this cash flow statement? Do the October and November balances indicate that you will have surplus cash to spend or save? Not necessarily! You must review total estimated spending over a longer period and reserve money to pay those expenses that occur irregularly, such as car maintenance, Christmas gifts, and so on. You must ensure that you do not spend cash that builds up during the year, unless you have used the **PEACE** system and it showed that you had a _genuine cash surplus_.

The cash flow statement is another key report we will use to prepare your budget. Ideally, we would wish to construct a cash flow statement for the twelve months of the upcoming budget period to see the timing of our projected spending.

_____

_____

_____

_____

_____

_____

_____

_____

Cash Flow Statement: Oct-Dec '98

INFLOWS	Oct	Nov	Dec	Total
Gross Salaries—Joshua & Rebecca	3150	3150	3150	9450
Less: Giving	(415)	(415)	(415)	(1245)
Less: Income Taxes & Other Deductions	(600)	(600)	(600)	(1800)
Less: Savings	(185)	(185)	(185)	(555)
Total Inflows	**1950**	**1950**	**1950**	**5850**
OUTFLOWS				
Capital Fund	150	150	150	450
Rent	500	500	500	1500
Car Expenses—Loan Repayment	300	300	300	900
Car Expenses—Gasoline	75	45	90	210
Car Expenses—Maintenance	0	0	90	90
Telephone	30	40	65	135
Entertainment & Recreation	125	160	200	485
Groceries	350	300	450	1100
Gifts	0	0	40	40
Total Outflows	**1530**	**1495**	**1885**	**4910**
Net Cash flow	**420**	**455**	**65**	**940**

Before projecting your cash flow, use the form on the next page to analyze your expenses for the past six months.

_____

_____

_____

_____

_____

_____

_____

_____

Cash Flow Statement: Past Six Months

Period:_____

INFLOWS							
Total Inflows							
OUTFLOWS							
Total Outflows							
Net Cash flow							

Next, project your cash flow for the next six months using the table on the next page before you start to prepare your budget.

_____

_____

_____

_____

_____

_____

Cash Flow Statement: Next Six Months

Period:_____

INFLOWS							
Total Inflows							
OUTFLOWS							
Total Outflows							
Net Cash flow							

[1] Market value is the amount someone may pay for an item today—not what you think it should be worth.

[2] Michel A. Bell, *Managing God's Money—The Basics*, (Belleville, Ontario: Essence Publishing, 2000), p. 43.

[3] Ibid, p. 43.

[4] Refer to page 49 of *Managing God's Money—The Basics*, for ideas to get out of debt.

Personal Notes

4

Jesus answered, "I am the way and the truth and the life.
No one comes to the Father except through me
(John 14:6 NIV).

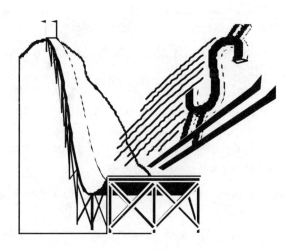

Critical Money Management Step #3
Establishing Life Goals

✶ ✶ ✶

Your "Destination"

Critical Money Management Step #3

(Establish Life Goals)

It's game seven of the Stanley Cup finals at the Molson Center in Montreal. The Vancouver Canucks meet the Montreal Canadiens with the series tied at 3-3. It's game time, and the players face-off. Montreal gets the puck, and in a series of brilliantly executed plays (yes, I am biased!), a Montreal player prepares to shoot the puck. Abruptly, he and all the other players start yelling at the referee! There are no nets on the ice! How do we score a goal? No nets, no goaltenders—what's the purpose of this game?

When you go through life without setting goals, how do you score a goal? The third step to managing God's money is to establish life goals. Your vital, eternal goal should be to develop a vibrant relationship with Jesus Christ. The corresponding "material" goal should be debt free living.

Life goals are essential because they do the following:

- Assist you to set priorities, both short-term and long-term; if you do not know where you wish to go, you will get there!
- Help to separate "needs" from "wants"; if you do not know how to separate needs from wants, money will control you as manufacturers seduce you with excellent advertising campaigns!
- Allow you to select the best alternative to fulfil your needs; if you do not set goals, you will lose options the closer you get to the event!

Goals require vision! Visions require faith! Faith comes from hearing and understanding the Word; it can move mountains! Establish your life goals now!

What is your vision for your life? Do you have a passion to create or design something? What are you good at? What do others say you are good at? What are the special gifts that Christ has given you:

- To play sports?
- In the Arts?
- In business?
- Other?

Pray and ask the Lord to show you your gifts. Discuss this subject with your pastor or trusted Christian friend. The bottom line is this: Try to identify a goal or goals. Submit (it) them to the Lord, and ask Him for His direction.

How many goals do you need? There is no fixed number. Do goals have to be financially based? No. If this is your first attempt at setting and implementing goals, you probably should restrict the number to a maximum of three essential ones. Your main focus should be where you sense the Lord directing you.

Use the Life Goal Form below to list your goals; it is self-explanatory. As you complete it, remember the three "C's" requirement for each goal: It must be **Clear, Complete, and Concise**. Further, in the future, you must be able to track actual progress or lack thereof against

the original goal. An example of an inappropriate goal would be this: "One day maybe I will
plete my university education." This has a built-in "out"—"one day." A more appropriate goal wo
be this: "Before age 35, I will complete my university education." That would be the ultimat.
goal—the destination! For this goal to be complete, you would "elaborate it" by specifying conditions that must be fulfilled to complete the university education, such as completing high school,
saving for the cost of fees and books and so on. The latter parameters would be your "Control
Items," for which you would prepare specific long-term goals and annual targets.

43. Read Exodus 4:10-13 and answer the following question:
43.1 Did Moses' speech impediment, about which he spoke, prevent God from using him?

_____

_____

_____

_____

44. Read 1 Samuel 17:31-54 and answer the following questions.
44.1 Was David an equal match for Goliath?

_____

_____

_____

_____

44.2 Although Goliath "appeared" to be better dressed for battle than David, did David
   express fear of Goliath?

_____

_____

_____

_____

44.3 Why was David not fearful?

_____

_____

_____

_____

**45. Is there something you sense the Lord wants you to do, but you are afraid to take
   the necessary step of faith to start the process? Explain.**

_____

_____

_____

_____

46. Read Hebrews Chapter 11 and list at least one event mentioned there that is similar to your situation.

_____

_____

_____

_____

47. Rewrite Proverbs 3:5-6 in your own words.

_____

_____

_____

_____

48. How are the verses in Hebrews 11 and Proverbs 3:5-6 relevant to your daily life?

_____

_____

_____

_____

49. Look back over the past month to see if you would act or react differently to any situation with your knowledge and acceptance of the Hebrews and Proverbs verses. Comment on this situation.

_____

_____

_____

_____

50. Read 2 Chronicles 20:1-30 and answer the following questions:
50.1 What was the problem (verse 1)?

_____

_____

_____

_____

50.2 What was the initial response (verse 3)?

_____

_____

_____

_____

50.3 What were the key elements of the prayer (verses 5-12)?

_____

_____

_____

_____

50.4 What was the answer (verses 13-17)?

_____

_____

_____

_____

50.5 How did they respond to God's answer (verses 18-19)?

_____

_____

_____

_____

50.6 What was the ultimate result (verses 20-30)?

_____

_____

_____

_____

50.7 What can we take away from 2 Chronicles 20:1-30 to apply to our daily lives?

_____

_____

_____

_____

51. **Read Philippians 3:8-14 and do the following:**
51.1 What is the basic message in these verses?

_____

_____

_____

_____

51.2 What do these verses tell you about looking back and having "pity parties"?

_____

_____

_____

_____

51.3 Are you prepared to accept the message in these verses as an "Eternal Life" Goal?

_____

_____

_____

_____

51.4 Write an "Eternal Life" Goal for yourself if your answer in 51.3 is "yes." If your answer is "no," explain why you can't accept the message.

_____

_____

_____

_____

_____

_____

_____

_____

_____

The following pages are two forms showing an example of a life goal with measurable targets being tracked. Review them, then prepare your life goals and targets. Ask someone you can trust to hold you accountable to track progress towards your life goals.

Life Goal Planning Sheet (LGPS)—Example

Many are the plans in the mind of a man, but it is the purpose of the Lord that will be established (Proverbs 19:21).

Name: Lofty Bimmer   **Period: Jan 2000 to Dec 2005**

Goal (Ultimate Destination) * * *	Elaboration of Goal
	Statement of Goal, including all prerequisites and subgoals. **(Must Satisfy Three "C's": Clear, Complete, Concise)**
Early Retirement	*Retire early after paying off mortgage; after saving for kids' education; and after identifying a second career.*

Control Items[1]	Ultimate Goal of Control Item (The Destination)[2]	Current Period's Target (Interim Checkpoint)[3]
Early Repayment of Mortgage	*Repay mortgage before age 50. At age 40 outstanding balance should not exceed $50,000. At age 45, outstanding balance should not exceed $20,000.*	*Accelerate monthly payment by $500. Pay 50% of all bonus or extra funds received towards mortgage.*
Education	*Total education cost to be saved by age 40.*	*Set aside at least $3000 annually*

Interim target at earlier age   **Target age for repayment**   **Specific targets for current year**

Life Goal Monitoring Sheet (LGMS)—Example

"Many are the plans in the mind of a man, but it is the purpose of the Lord that will be established" (Proverbs 19:21).

Name: Lofty Bimmer   **Period:** Jan 2000 to Dec 2005

COMPARISON OF ACTUAL PROGRESS TOWARDS ACHIEVING GOALS AGAINST PLANNED PROGRESS

Goal (Ultimate Destination) * * * *Early Retirement*	**Elaboration of Goal** Precise statement of Goal, including all prerequisites. **(Must Satisfy Three "Cs": Clear, Complete, Concise)** *Retire early after paying off mortgage; after saving for kids' education; and after identifying a second career.*
Control Item[4] (From LGPS) **Control Item Goal** (From LGPS)	*Early Repayment of Mortgage* *Repay mortgage before age 50. At age 40 outstanding balance should not exceed $50,000. At age 45, outstanding balance should not exceed $20,000.*
Date of Review *31 December 1999*	**Comparison of Progress Against Goal** *Actual balance outstanding $55,000. $5,000 less than original goal.*
31 January 2000	*Mortgage payments are ahead of plan, but interest rates are increasing. Consider increasing rate of principal reduction in March 2000. Mortgage balance is still $5000 less than original. Mortgage renewal in March 2000.*

What is impossible with men is possible with God (Luke 18:27 NIV).

Life Goal Planning Sheet (LGPS)

*Many are the plans in the mind of a man, but it is the purpose
of the Lord that will be established (Proverbs 19:21).*

Name: Period:

Goal (Ultimate Destination)	Elaboration of Goal Statement of Goal, including all prerequisites, and subgoals. **(Must Satisfy Three "C's": Clear, Complete, Concise)**	
Control Items	**Ultimate Goal of Control Item** (The Destination)	**Current Period's Target** (Interim Checkpoint)

Life Goal Monitoring Sheet (LGMS)

Many are the plans in the mind of a man, but it is the purpose
of the Lord that will be established (Proverbs 19:21).

Name: Period:

COMPARISON OF ACTUAL PROGRESS TOWARDS ACHIEVING GOALS AGAINST PLANNED PROGRESS

Goal (Ultimate Destination)	Elaboration of Goal Precise statement of Goal, including all prerequisites. **(Must Satisfy Three "C's": Clear, Complete, Concise)**
Control Item (From LGPS) **Control Item Goal** (From LGPS)	
Date of Review	**Comparison of Progress Against Goal**

What is impossible with men is possible with God (Luke 18:27 NIV).

[1] A "Control Item" is a specific element of your life goal to be monitored. It is a stage of your journey toward your goal. A goal of a healthy lifestyle may have jogging or weight loss as a control item. Use one form per control item.

[2] "Goal of Control Item" is the "destination" of the Control Item. For a healthy lifestyle, it could be losing 30 pounds over six months.

[3] "Current Period's Target" could be the loss of five pounds monthly (period): sometimes "Goal" and "Target" are the same.

[4] Use one form per control item. For a goal of a healthy lifestyle, this form could track progress for the "loss of weight" control item.

Personal Notes

5

I know what it is to be in need, and I know what it is to have plenty.
I have learned the secret of being content in any and every situation.
whether well fed or hungry, whether living in plenty or in want
(Philippians 4:12 NIV).

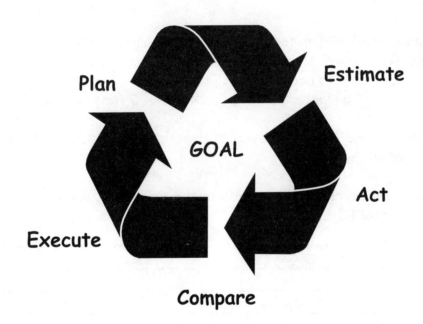

Plan

Estimate

GOAL

Execute

Act

Compare

The PEACE Budgetary Control System

The PEACE Budgetary Control System

The PEACE Budgetary Control System allows you to achieve **goals** systematically in the following manner:

- **Plan** for a specific period to accomplish precise **goals**.
- **Estimate** and record the expenses needed to achieve those **goals**.
- **Act** on the plan and record actual results as you progress toward your **goals**.
- **Compare** actual results with the plan and with the estimated expenses required to attain the **goals**.
- **Execute** changes necessary to remain on course to realize the **goals**.

After you set your **life goals**, start the **PEACE** Budgetary Control System which is predicated on the following:

> **Goals** (your destination—trip to Vancouver) that translate into…
>> **Plans** (how you will get there) the cost of which you…
>>> **Estimate** to become…
>>>> **Budget** allocations (such as $300 for transportation)

Remember, today is your "present." Open it! Experience it! Use it to the maximum because tomorrow you may not get another!

52. Read Exodus Chapters 3-12 and answer the following questions:

52.1 What was the **goal** (Chapter 3:10)?

_____

_____

_____

_____

52.2 What was the **plan** (Chapter 3:12-22)?

_____

_____

_____

_____

52.3 Did the **plan** change in the process of accomplishing the **goal**? How? (Chapter 4)

_____

_____

_____

_____

52.4 What were the key obstacles to implementing the **plan**? (Chapter 5:6-7; 21-22; Chapter 6:30)

_____

_____

_____

_____

52.5 Did the **goal** change?

_____

_____

_____

_____

52.6 What can you take from Exodus 3-12 to help you achieve your **goals**?

_____

_____

_____

_____

53. **Read Luke 14:28-33 and answer these questions:**
53.1 What is the cost of following Jesus Christ?

_____

_____

_____

_____

53.2 Do you agree that you should **"count" or "estimate" the cost** (verse 28) involved in all activities before you start?

_____

_____

_____

_____

53.3 How can you apply this approach (verse 28) to your **life goals** and to your **budget**?

_____

_____

_____

_____

53.4 List the hindrances to applying verse 28 to your daily walk. Ask the Lord to help you remove them.

_____

_____

_____

_____

The **PEACE** Budget Computation Form[1] **(PBCF)** below shows gross monthly salary at $3150, from which **you deduct your giving first**—before taxes and other payroll deductions! Develop this mindset of giving first, even before the government takes its share from your salary! To complete the income section, deduct **savings** and **capital fund**[2] amounts from gross income. Then determine the net balance to allocate to the various expense categories in the expense section of PBCF. This example reflects $1800 available for allocation for monthly expenses.

Before addressing **giving**, **savings**, and **capital fund**, let's look at one option that could encourage you to stick with the **PEACE** Budgetary Control System once you have started: becoming accountable to someone.

Establishing Accountability

Establish accountability to help you to implement and to follow the **PEACE** system. Accountability is entrenched in many successful businesses. It is answering to someone for your actions. Usually governments and individuals do not practise it.

54. **Read Matthew 25:14-30 and answer the following questions:**
54.1 As Christians, to whom are we accountable?

_____

_____

_____

_____

54.2 For what are we accountable?

_____

_____

_____

_____

55. Read Galatians 6:2 and answer the following questions:

55.1 To whom are we accountable?

_____

_____

_____

_____

55.2 Why should we "carry each other's burdens"?

_____

_____

_____

_____

55.3 Rewrite this verse in your own words.

_____

_____

_____

_____

Choose someone trustworthy, with whom you feel comfortable, to hold you accountable. You don't need to give him or her all the details of your affairs. Give him or her the right to ask a simple question: "Have you been following the **PEACE** system?" Remember, you are spending God's money, and you are accountable to Jesus!

Giving Is the First "Deduction" from Your Income!

56. **Would the owner of a business give his manager 90% of the profits from the business and retain 10% only? Yes or no? _____**

57. **Are you happy with the amount you give to the Lord's work? Yes or no? _____**

58. **Explain your answer to 57.**

_____

_____

_____

_____

59. **Should you be giving more or less? _____**

60. **Read Mark 12:41-44 and answer the following questions:**

60.1 Did the widow give a "tithe" (10% of her income) or more?

_____

_____

_____

_____

60.2 Explain Malachi 3:8-10 in the context of your giving.

_____

_____

_____

_____

61. **Read 2 Corinthians 9:6-8 and do the following:**
61.1 Rewrite these verses in your own words.

_____

_____

_____

_____

61.2 Reflect on items 56-61; pray and ask the Lord to direct your future giving. Write a goal for your future giving.

_____

_____

_____

_____

Savings

Genesis 40 and 41 portray an excellent biblical example of respect for God and saving for a future event. God revealed to Pharaoh in a dream that there would be seven years of abundance followed by seven years of famine in Egypt. Because Joseph explained the dream, Pharaoh put him in charge of Egypt to implement God's plan. **For seven years, Joseph systematically stored excess food.** The next seven years of drought, Egypt had enough food!

Learn to save regularly at least three to five percent of gross salary from each salary cheque. This is additional to contributions to your Registered Retirement Savings Plan (RRSP[3]) and to your company's registered pension plan. Abide by these guidelines:

- Do not use regular savings (this 3-5%) to supplement your household budget.
- Maximize your annual pension and RRSP contributions.
- Consider regular savings as payroll deductions. Indeed, arrange for automatic transfer to your bank, if possible.

Later, regular savings will provide the base for prudent investing.

62. **What are three factors that tend to prevent us from saving?**

_____

_____

_____

_____

63. **What can we learn from Genesis 41 to help us counteract the factors in 62?**

_____

_____

_____

_____

Capital Fund

Consider the **capital fund** as targeted savings: savings geared toward specific future expenses. Usually, individuals do not plan to purchase cars, refrigerators, stoves, carpets, heat pumps, and other major equipment. They buy them as needed, and often they use credit. Similarly, when they need to repair or replace these items, they use funds from the household budget, which means they must forego some other expense item. Generally, they borrow. This ad hoc asset replacement and asset maintenance can be stressful and expensive.

I suggest that all individuals and couples copy corporations and systematically provide for replacing and repairing capital equipment. Accordingly, accumulate funds systematically in a **capital fund** to finance major purchases and large maintenance expenses. Implementing this will eliminate crises from your annual budgets.

Individuals and couples, who attend my seminars and whom I have counselled, testify repeatedly that the **capital fund** had the greatest positive impact on their finances. You need a **capital fund** to become and to remain **debt free**. Ultimately, you can plan your major purchases for which you will pay cash. You will pay cash also from the **capital fund** for unplanned repairs and maintenance expenses as they occur.

Ideally, start a **capital fund** in your early teens. Therefore encourage your teenagers to start their **fund** now, contributing regularly at least 50% of all income received.

Allocate at least 5% of your gross income to your **capital fund**.[4] Initially, the exact percentage is not critical; development of habitual contribution to the **fund is key**.

At your next salary increase, and whenever you get unexpected funds, to the extent you do not give these funds away, place them in your **capital fund**. Continue saving this amount for at least twelve months. Keep building this account until the **fund** is large enough to meet relevant planned and unexpected expenses mentioned above. Thereafter, as the **fund** grows, you will develop a base for more "aggressive" giving and prudent investing.

Where should you keep the **capital fund**? In a savings account? On fixed deposit? It depends on the size of the **fund**! Initially place your deposits where you can access them quickly, like a money market account.[5] As it grows, use other short-term investment vehicles. Consult an independent financial adviser to guide you. However, do not buy stocks or bonds, which are long-term investment instruments. **The capital fund** deposits are additional to your savings and your contingency budget.

It is never too late to start to accumulate funds in a **capital fund**. Start today so that you will not borrow to replace and repair your major assets! Identify the items for which you will set aside funds in your **capital fund** monthly and list them in the Table below:

Capital Fund: Monthly Allocation

Item Description	$	Comments

As needed, withdraw amounts from the **capital fund** to pay for specific repairs and major purchases that you anticipated and provided for in the **capital fund.**

_____

_____

_____

_____

_____

_____

_____

PEACE Budget Computation Form (PBCF): Income—Example

Eternal Goal:

"I want to know Christ and the power of his resurrection and the fellowship of sharing in his sufferings, becoming like him in his death" (Philippians 3:10 NIV).

Material Goals:

1. Accumulate Down Payment On Home In 3 years
2. Balanced Budget Every Year
3. Vacation Overseas Next Year

Budget Categories	Frequency of Income/Expenses			Monthly Budget
	Weekly	Monthly	Yearly	
Salary		3150		3150
Less: Giving		(415)		(415)
Less: Taxes		(600)		(600)
Less: Savings		(185)		(185)
Less: Capital Fund		(150)		(150)
Net Salary		1800		1800

_____

_____

_____

_____

_____

_____

_____

PEACE Budget Computation Form: Expenses—Example

Budget Categories	Frequency of Income/Expenses			Monthly Budget (1800)
	Weekly	Monthly	Yearly	
Rent		500		500
Car Expenses				
Loan Repayment		300		300
Gasoline	15 ◄	x 4=	►	60
Maintenance			360	
Groceries	100 ◄	x 4=	►	400
Entertainment & Recreation				
Meals	50			200
Video Rental	20			80
Movies	10			40
Telephone		50		50
Clothing			480 ◄ ÷ 12 =	40
Gifts				
Birthdays			60	5
Christmas			120	10
Contingency	21			85
Total Expenses	216	850	1020	1800

Don't be surprised when you finish allocating budgeted amounts, that your total expenses represent twice your available income; a common first budget result. Now the fun begins as you start the inevitable "cutting" exercise! **Before finalizing the budget, go exploring!**

Review the following areas, and you may find available funds:

- Cable/Telephone/Internet charges
- Entertainment/Eating out/Daily lunch expenses
- Bank charges/Credit card interest
- Insurance premiums
- Car lease payments
- Gifts/Vacation expenses

Compute your budget using the blank forms on the following pages.

PEACE Budget Computation Form (PBCF): Incomes

Eternal Goals:
"I want to know Christ and the power of his resurrection and the fellowship of sharing in his sufferings, becoming like him in his death" (Philippians 3:10 NIV).

Material Goals:
1.
2.
3.

Budget Categories	Frequency of Income/Expenses			Monthly Budget
	Weekly	Monthly	Yearly	
Salary				
Less: Giving				
Less: Taxes				
Less: Savings				
Less: Capital Fund				
Net Salary				

_____

_____

_____

_____

_____

_____

_____

PEACE Budget Computation Form: Expenses

Budget Categories	Frequency of Income/Expenses			Monthly Budget
	Weekly	Monthly	Yearly	
Contingency				
Total Expenses				

Before spending, transfer **monthly budgeted amounts** from the **PBCF** above to the appropriate section of the **PEACE** Budget Worksheet ("**PBW**") below.

_____

_____

_____

_____

_____

_____

PEACE Budget Worksheet (PBW)—Example

Sept '98	Description	Total	Rent	Car Loan	Gasoline	Car Repairs	Groceries	Meals	Video	Movies	Telephone	Clothes	Birthdays	Christmas	Contingency
1	Allocation Sep	1800	500	300	60	30	400	200	80	40	50	40	5	10	85
	Rent	500	500												
4	Lunch	35						35							
	Balance Left	1265	0	300	60	30	400	165	80	40	50	40	5	10	85
7	Provigo Supermarket	179					179								
	Balance Left	1086	0	300	60	30	221	165	80	40	50	40	5	10	85
9	Cinema/Telephone	30								15	15				
	Balance Left	1056	0	300	60	30	221	165	80	25	35	40	5	10	85
11	Shell Gas Station	25			25										
	Balance Left	1031	0	300	35	30	221	165	80	25	35	40	5	10	85
13	Royal Bank	300		300											
	Balance Left	731	0	0	35	30	221	165	80	25	35	40	5	10	85
15	Dinner	75						75							
	Balance Left	656	0	0	35	30	221	90	80	25	35	40	5	10	85
17	Provigo	150					150								
	Balance Left	506	0	0	35	30	71	90	80	25	35	40	5	10	85
21	Shell	15			15										
	Balance Left	491	0	0	20	30	71	90	80	25	35	40	5	10	85
23	Video	30							30						
	Balance Left	461	0	0	20	30	71	90	50	25	35	40	5	10	85
23	Provigo	100					100								
	Balance Left	361	0	0	20	30	-29	90	50	25	35	40	5	10	85
27	Sears	76										76			
	Balance Left	285	0	0	20	30	-29	90	50	25	35	-36	5	10	85
29	Telephone	30									30				
30	Balance Left	255	0	0	20	30	-29	90	50	25	5	-36	5	10	85
30	Budget Oct 1998	1800	500	300	60	30	400	200	80	40	50	40	5	10	85
	Allocation Oct	2055	500	300	80	60	371	290	130	65	55	4	10	20	170

"The things impossible with men are possible with God" (Luke 18:27).

We carry forward the balance at the end of the month because actual spending is not normally spread evenly over the period like the budget allocation. However, save surplus budget allocations.

Before spending any amount, whether by cash, cheque, or credit card, check the PBW for the available budget. After spending, enter required details of the transaction on the PBW. Deduct each expense first from the budget for the month, then from the balance left.

PEACE Budget Worksheet (PBW)

DATE:	Description	Total													
	Budget Month:														

[1] The principles to determine your budget are the same if you use a computerized system. In both, you need to understand your spending pattern, and you need to estimate your future expenses that are necessary to achieve your goals.

[2] Capital Fund: An account maintained to finance major purchases and large maintenance expenses to eliminate crises from annual budgets and to enable planning and scheduling of necessary major maintenance and major purchases.

[3] As I stated in *Managing God's Money—The Basics* (p. 163), a Registered Retirement Savings Plan (RRSP) is a "...great opportunity to save and earn a significant return on your savings! Each situation is unique so consult a financial adviser to determine your actual RRSP Entitlement...." An RRSP allows you to save income earned today to a maximum annual amount, without tax being deducted.

Another excellent saving vehicle is an RESP (Registered Educational Savings Plan). This is a savings vehicle generally used by parents to save for their children's post-secondary education. Effectively, it is an agreement between an individual and a person or organization whereby the individual makes contributions that accumulate tax-free in an account for the benefit of a beneficiary or beneficiaries (such as his child). The contributing individual does not get a tax deduction for contributions. Beneficiaries use funds to pay for education expenses.

Here is the situation as of October 2000:

- Annual contribution limits and lifetime limits depend on the calendar year. The annual limit for 1997 and future years is $4,000. The lifetime limit for 1996 and future years is $42,000. These limits apply to each beneficiary, regardless of the number of plans for that particular beneficiary.

- Since 1998 the Ministry Of Human Resources Development will pay a 20% Canada Education Savings Grant on the first $2000 of annual contributions made to all eligible RESPs of a qualifying beneficiary.

I encourage you to (a) visit Canada Customs and Revenue Agency's Web site for more details of RRSPs and RESPs, and (b) review your situation with an independent financial adviser.

[4] For replacement items such as a fridge or stove, I compute my capital fund allocation by dividing the estimated replacement cost by the estimated useful life. Thus if I estimate the combined replacement cost of a fridge and stove at $3000 and the useful life at 10 years, I set aside $25 per month (3000 divided by 10=300 divided by 12=$25). For combined major repairs in the home, to the car etc., of $1500 every two years, I would set aside $62.50 per month (1500 divided by 2=750 divided by 12=$62.50). Monthly, I would transfer $87.50 ($25+62.50) to a money market account. When repairs and replacement become necessary, I transfer the funds from the money market. Consequently, my monthly budget is undisturbed!

[5] A money market account, generally, is a safe and accessible account that you can operate with a financial institution. Funds in this account are invested predominantly in Treasury Bills (loans to the government). The interest rate that you earn is higher than on regular bank deposits. Generally, you need to give 48 hours notice to withdraw the funds.

Personal Notes

6

By contrast, the fruit of the Spirit is love, joy, peace, patience, kindness, generosity, faithfulness, gentleness, and self-control. There is no law against such things. And those who belong to Christ Jesus have crucified the flesh with its passions and desires. If we live by the Spirit, let us also be guided by the Spirit. Let us not become conceited, competing against one another, envying one another (Galatians 5:22-26 NRSV).

The Control Phase of PEACE
(Implementing Three Spending Aids)

* * *

The GAS Principle
The PLANE Spending Analysis
The AFFORDABILITY Index

Before committing to major expenditures[1] (you decide what's major—be realistic!) apply these three spending aids. They are your prime control mechanisms in the **control** phase of the **PEACE** system:

- The **GAS** Principle ("**GAS**")
- The **PLANE** Spending Analysis ("**PLANE**")
- The **AFFORDABILITY** Index

GAS is the foundation of the **PEACE** Budgetary Control System. It is essential to manage God's money effectively. Before I explain its application, here is a recap:

The GAS Principle

Key Truth #1: God Owns Everything (Psalm 24:1, Colossians 1:16).
Key Truth #2: Accept What You Have (1 Timothy 6:7-8, Hebrews 13:5).
Key Truth #3: Seek First His Kingdom And Submit Your Requests To Him (Matthew 6:33, Proverbs 19:21).

To apply the **GAS** principle to your proposed expenses, ask the questions below **before** you **commit** to spend.

Application of Key Truth #1 (God Owns Everything)

- Will the spending decision directly or indirectly **conflict** with Jesus' teaching in the Bible?
- For example, will it **promote** or **condone** abortion, hate, greed, lust, or sexual immorality?

I call these questions the **external** drivers of **GAS**. They focus on the **nature** of expenditures. I am not suggesting that you become paranoid, trying to trace the final sources of all your spending! I am reminding you that it's God's money you are managing, not yours. Consequently, you should not knowingly spend funds that ultimately will dishonour Jesus. Your spending must reflect your beliefs as a Christian!

64. Read 1 Corinthians 6:9-11 and answer the following questions:
64.1 Rewrite these verses in your own words.

_____

_____

_____

_____

64.2 Before spending major funds, what (if any) information should you try to obtain about the nature of the expense and about the company selling the goods or service?

_____

_____

64.3 Should you be concerned about the company and the **nature** of the expense?

_____

_____

_____

_____

Application of Key Truth #2 (Accept What You Have)

- Am I being selfish?
- Am I being greedy?
- Am I just keeping up with the Joneses?

These are the **internal** drivers. They focus on **you** and your **motives**. Even if the contemplated expenditure honours Christ (more accurately, it does not dishonour Him), you must examine your heart and understand your motives for spending. Another helpful question is this: **Am I accumulating things that are nice to have but not necessary?**

65. **Read Luke 12:15-21 and answer these questions:**
65.1 Define "greed."

_____

_____

_____

_____

65.2 How do you assess if you are merely keeping up with the Joneses?

_____

_____

_____

_____

65.3 Do these verses mean you should not save? You should have no possessions? Explain.

_____

_____

_____

_____

65.4 Explain Matthew 25:15-30 in the context of Key Truth # 2.

_____

_____

_____

_____

66. **Accepting what we have means the following:**

- We accept the abilities we have been given and we stop complaining about our perceived inadequacies.
- We do not look at what our neighbour has as a benchmark for what we should have.
- We do the best with the talent and resources that we have.
- We work to the best of our abilities, not because we like our jobs, but because we were commanded to do so by our Lord….
- We acknowledge that we have time to do what God has called us to do for His glory
  - …there is enough time to do everything that is important!
  - …identify what is important and do it!
  - …don't borrow to get what you want but do not need.

66.1 Do you agree with statements in item 66? Explain.

_____

_____

_____

Application of Key Truth #3
(Seek First His Kingdom And Submit Your Requests to Him)

- How is my walk with God?
- Have I been feeding on His Word?
- Have I prayed and sought to know God's will?

These are the **eternal** drivers. They are the bottom line! They focus on your Walk.

The Bible does not promise you material riches if you do God's will. It promises blessings! You will know the form of blessings only when you receive them! That's good enough for me, how about you?

I encourage you to reflect on the **GAS** principle. Sure it requires effort and time. I assure you that if you decide to walk with Jesus and live a holy life, it is merely one aspect of such a life. The **GAS** principle is not about financial analysis alone; it is stewardship in action!

67. **Explain Romans 12:2 in your own words:**

_____

_____

_____

_____

67.1 Do you invest in "quiet time" to listen to Jesus' voice? Do you speak to Him often?

_____

_____

_____

_____

67.2 Do you receive the Word eagerly and examine it daily like the Bereans in Acts 17:11? Explain.

_____

_____

_____

_____

68. **Read Matthew 7:7-12. Rewrite these verses in your own words.**

_____

_____

_____

_____

_____

_____

_____

68.1 Do these verses mean that anything you "want" you will get by asking?

_____

_____

_____

_____

68.2 What conditions (if any) should exist to be confident we will receive what we ask for?

_____

_____

_____

_____

68.3 Do the verses mention a time frame for us to receive our requests?

_____

_____

_____

_____

PLANE Spending Analysis

Why do we need another set of questions? Why isn't the **GAS** principle adequate? The **PLANE analysis** complements the **GAS principle**; use them sequentially. If the result of the **GAS** analysis is negative, do not proceed to the **PLANE**. **(If there is no GAS you can't fly!)**

The first two sets of questions of the **GAS** principle focus on **external** and **internal** drivers: they are concerned with **what** and **why**. The **PLANE analysis**, on the other hand, goes further and deals with the following:

- **Why Now**—Did you plan it?
- **How**—How will you pay for it?
- **Alternatives**—Are there alternatives available?
- **Necessity**—Do you truly need it?
- **Effectiveness**—Is this the most effective use of God's resources now?

The third set of questions (the third Key Truth) of the **GAS** principle applies equally to the **PLANE** analysis. Indeed, think of PLANES! Followed systematically, the **PLANE** and the **Affordability Index** will keep you out of debt. Here are the **PLANE** questions:

- **P**   Did I **Plan** this expenditure and did I include it in my budget?
- **L**   Will the expenditure increase my **Loans**?
- **A**   Are there realistic **Alternatives** to achieve my spending objective?
- **N**   Is the expenditure **Necessary** to achieve my spending objective?
- **E**   Is this the most **Effective** use of resources now, relative to my **life goals and budget goals**?

Underpinning the **PLANE** analysis is this: Every spending decision has a **basic objective** that you should identify in your evaluation. If you decided to buy a new bicycle, you should know the reason for the purchase. Is it to enter a special race during the summer, for outdoor exercise, or for a different reason?

The Affordability Index

I designed this **index** so specific situations would produce particular results. Thus, I chose the numbers in the table. Scores are either zero, two, four, or six—nothing else. You can't score one, three, five, or seven. Below are questions to answer as you complete the **affordability index.** Also below is an example of the process you would follow to decide if you should buy a bicycle to enter a bicycle race during the summer; review these comments in conjunction with the **affordability index** below.

Plan

In the Budget or Can Be Accommodated	0
Out of the Budget and Cannot Be Accommodated	2

An item is **in the plan** if a specific allocation was made when the original budget was prepared (ideally, before the start of the budget period). If you change your **plan** to buy that specific item, the original budget allocated for that item is frozen automatically. However, that amount is available to "accommodate" purchasing an item, of equivalent or lesser value, to which you apply the **affordability index.** For example, if you **planned** to buy a CD player and included $150 in the original **budget,** this amount is available for a CD player **only**! If you are not going to buy the CD player, this $150 is **frozen and not available** for any other item. You changed your plans; the money is **no longer available** in the budget!

Suppose, subsequently, you wish to buy a bicycle for $150 and you had not included this in your original plan and budget. It may be "accommodated" in the plan (because you no longer will buy the CD player), provided your total actual expenses for the budget period will not exceed your total budgeted expenses for that period. For example, if your budget for the year was $20,000 and you estimate now that you will spend less than $19,850, you may accommodate the purchase of the bicycle for $150. Otherwise you may not.

• If the bicycle was in the plan, score **zero**[2]. Also if it was not in the plan but can be accommodated—as in our example above—score **zero**. Otherwise, score **two**.

Loans

Unchanged	0
Increase	6

To buy this bicycle will your **loans** increase? Score **zero** if your loans will not increase and **six** if they will. It does not matter if you planned and budgeted for this purchase! The test here is based strictly on the change in your total loans, including credit card purchases. **A credit card charge will score a six unless you have sufficient funds in your bank account to cover the charge and you plan to pay the balance in full when due.** The PEACE system teaches you to strive to be debt free. The **Affordability Index** captures this and penalizes all borrowing. I will discuss one exception later: purchasing a car that you need to earn your living.

Alternative

None	0
Yes	2

Is there a realistic **alternative** to achieve the **spending objective**? ...not necessarily an alternative bicycle, just an alternative to achieve the objective. If your objective was to enter a bicycle race, the viable alternative would be a different type of bicycle. If the objective were outdoor exercise, the realistic alternative could be walking or jogging, depending on other factors. Do not be concerned now with an alternative-spending objective; this is not the focus of the **affordability index.** Once you progress to using the **affordability index**, already you have decided to buy the item: it has passed the **GAS** principle! This analysis is to determine if you can "afford" to buy the item. Score **two** for a realistic alternative and **zero** if none.

Why do you score any points if there is a realistic alternative? Doesn't this penalize you? Sure it does. If there is a realistic alternative, perform a separate analysis on the **affordability index** and compare results.

Necessary

Yes	0
No	4

Is the bicycle or the alternative identified **necessary** to achieve the **spending objective**? If your answer is yes, score a **zero**, if no, score a **four**.

Effective

Yes	0
No	6

For this fifth question, it is your **life goals and budget goals** that are relevant, **not the spending objective**. Is this the most effective use of resources relative to your life and budget goals now? You may ask this question another way: Will this amount reduce the amount needed to achieve a **life** or **budget goal**? For example, if a budget goal was to eliminate credit card balances, will this expense reduce cash available to achieve that goal? If it will not, score a **zero**; if it will, score a **six**. Apart from the **Vase (see below)**, you can't "afford" an item on which spending is not the most effective use of resources!

Apart from two exceptions, you cannot **afford** an item if one or more of the following are true:

· If you have to **borrow** to buy it.
· If spending to buy it is not the most **effective** use of resources.
· If you did not **plan** the expenditure and it is not **necessary**.

The table on the next page shows six different spending decisions—each with a different result. The microwave scored a perfect zero (you get the total score by adding the five high-lighted answers). It was planned; it did not increase your loans; there were no practical alternatives to reheat quickly; it was necessary now; and this was the most effective use of resources now. The opposite was true for the boat.

The Affordability Index—Example

Spending Decisions	Micro-wave	Suit	University Course	Vase*	Car	Boat
Objective of Spending	Quick Reheat	Work	Self Improve-ment	Specific Vacation	Work	Recre-ation
PLAN						
In or Can Be Accomodated	O	O	O	O	O	O
Out & Cannot Be Accomodated	2	2	2	2	2	2
LOANS						
Unchanged	O	O	O	O	O	O
Increase	6	6	6	6	6	6
ALTERNATIVE						
None	O	O	O	O	O	O
Yes	2	2	2	2	2	2
NECESSARY						
Yes	O	O	O	O	O	O
No	4	4	4	4	4	4
EFFECTIVE						
Yes	O	O	O	O	O	O
No	6	6	6	6	6	6
TOTAL of Highlighted Numbers	0	4	4	8	8	20
	← Affordable →			Special Case	Special Case	Not Affordable

The Affordability Index Scoring Regime

Scores	Results
< 6	You can afford the item
6 & above (except for a vase and a car)	You can't afford the item
8 or less	• You can afford the item as a vase • You may buy a car under specific conditions

The Affordability Index

Spending Decisions						
Objective of Spending						
PLAN						
In or Can Be Accomodated	0	0	0	0	0	0
Out & Cannot Be Accomodated	2	2	2	2	2	2
LOANS						
Unchanged	0	0	0	0	0	0
Increase	6	6	6	6	6	6
ALTERNATIVE						
None	0	0	0	0	0	0
Yes	2	2	2	2	2	2
NECESSARY						
Yes	0	0	0	0	0	0
No	4	4	4	4	4	4
EFFECTIVE						
Yes	0	0	0	0	0	0
No	6	6	6	6	6	6
TOTAL of Highlighted Numbers						

Scores	Results
< 6	You can afford the item
6 & above (except for a vase and a car)	You can't afford the item
8 or less	• You can afford the item as a vase • You may buy a car under specific conditions

The Affordability Index and the Vase

Several years ago, my wife introduced this concept into our planning and budgeting. She believed we were too inflexible in our allocations. She insisted that "we break a **Vase**" periodically and spend discretionary funds under specific conditions. She cited John 12:3-7 as the basis for the **vase**:

> Mary took a pound of costly perfume made of pure nard, anointed Jesus' feet, and wiped them with her hair. The house was filled with the fragrance of the perfume. But Judas Iscariot, one of his disciples (the one who was about to betray him), said, "Why was this perfume not sold for three hundred denarii and the money given to the poor?" (He said this not because he cared about the poor, but because he was a thief; he kept the common purse and used to steal what was put into it.) Jesus said, "Leave her alone. She bought it so that she might keep it for the day of my burial...."

Mary's sacrifice is key to this story. She chose to use this expensive perfume to anoint Jesus' feet instead of using it for herself. To include a **vase** in your budget, you must be following strictly the **GAS principle**, and its supporting cast of the **PEACE** system and **PLANE** analysis. Further, you must sacrifice!

To "break a **vase**," you would have scored eight or less on the **affordability index**, which meant the following:

- The item is included **in the plan** and **in the budget initially**. Thus, the concept of **"not in the plan but can be accommodated" does not apply**. Accordingly, the expenditure must be agreed when you prepare the plan.
- Your **loans** will **not increase**.
- There **is** (usually) an **alternative**.
- The expense **is necessary** to achieve the spending objective, but
- It **is not** the most **effective** use of resources.

This is the only instance in which Doreen and I consider purchasing an item knowing that spending on that specific item is not the most effective use of resources at the time. Usually, therein lies the sacrifice; you forego achieving a **life goal** for a discretionary expenditure! Generally, a **vase** applied to a special vacation that we have taken. When we went to Israel in 1989, we knew that we had to defer some specific goals.

We use these additional guidelines before we implement the **vase**:

- We must have been following rigorously the **GAS**, **PLANE** and **PEACE** systems.
- We allow no more than one **vase** per year (however, we do not implement one **Vase** every year).
- We must be in total agreement with all aspects of the decision.

The Affordability Index and the Purchase of a Car

Initially, I was not convinced that anyone should borrow to buy a car. However, Bill (my son-in-law) and Doreen convinced me; after careful research, I added this exception. Scoring eight or less on the **affordability index** means also that you may purchase a car under certain conditions:

- You need the car to earn your living,
- There is no alternative,
- Your loans will increase, but
- This is the most effective use of resources.

Jonah graduated from university as an engineer. He has a job, but there is no public transport to take him to work. Taking taxis and buses during the week and renting a car (if needed) on week-ends would be cumbersome and expensive. **His only choice was to borrow money to buy a second-hand car.**

If you decide to buy a car with a loan, you should adhere to the following guidelines:

- Don't buy a new car—you are likely to get the greatest value from a one/two-year-old car.
- Develop a plan to pay off the loan over a short period.
- Start the **GAS**, **PEACE**, and **PLANE** systems.
- Use the **affordability index** systematically.

Finally, in addition to the spending aids discussed above, you should try to develop specific habits to help you control your spending. Here are some tips:

Spending Tips

- **Do** remember that God provides, always, all the resources you **need**, which may be less than what you **want**!

- **Do** spend only when you know that spending is God's will for you. Ask the Lord to give you a verse of scripture to confirm your "feelings." Before you spend, check the **PEACE Budget Worksheet** to see the allocation. If you have none left, maybe you can't spend.

- Shop around before buying; visit second-hand stores.

- Always read the fine print before signing any document.

- If a "deal" seems too good to be true, **it is too good** to be true!
  - Why would a company give you a gift without strings? What's in it for them?

- When you receive a raise or additional income, first allocate your tithe and extra giving, then allocate the balance to the **capital fund**.

- Spend because there is a need!

- **Don't** spend impulsively.

- When the urge comes, wait at least 24 to 48 hours and ensure that you apply the **GAS**, the **PLANE** and **affordability index.**

- **Don't** spend just because you have money.

- **Don't** go shopping **without** a list.

- **Don't** buy anything other than what is on the list.

- **Don't** visit garage sales unless to buy specific budgeted items.

- **Don't** be enticed by **sales.**

- You benefit from a sale only if you need the item you purchased. Seventy five percent off is 25% too much if you do not need the item!

- **Don't** upgrade your home, your car, or "grown-up toys," unless you use the **GAS** the **PLANE** and the **affordability index**

- **Don't** be embarrassed to negotiate prices.

- **Don't** use a credit card unless you have the funds in the bank.

- A credit card is a cheque that is cleared in about 30 days

- If you can't pay your credit card balance in full every month, stop using it!

- **Don't** borrow, except to buy a home—save for other items.

- If you wish to borrow to maximize your RRSP contribution, you should repay the loan in full immediately when you receive your tax refund. Otherwise, **don't** borrow.

---

[1] The analyses refer equally to spending on goods, services and other intangibles.

[2] Highlight the box on the **Affordability Index** with the correct score.

Personal Notes

_____

_____

_____

_____

_____

_____

_____

_____

_____

_____

_____

_____

_____

_____

_____

_____

_____

_____

_____

_____

_____

_____

_____

7

Train a child in the way he should go,
and when he is old he will not turn from it

(Proverbs 22:6 NIV).

Couples and Children

Couples

The Apostle Paul, in 2 Corinthians 6:14 says this: "Do not be mismatched with unbelievers. For what partnership is there between righteousness and lawlessness? Or what fellowship is there between light and darkness?"

69. **Rewrite 2 Corinthians 6:14 in your own words.**

_____

_____

_____

_____

70. **What is the source of values for a Christian couple?**

_____

_____

_____

_____

71. **Read 1 Corinthians 7:12-14 and rewrite it in your own words.**

_____

_____

_____

_____

Here are some issues you should agree on before you enter, and during, a marriage relationship:

- How do you set your **life goals** and budget goals?
- How do you treat **assets that each brings into the marriage?** Do the assets enter one pool owned jointly or will they be separate? What about loans and other liabilities? Will they be assumed equally?
- How do you **title property** acquired after marriage? This is essential if the wife decides to be a stay-at-home mom to raise the children. I know men who refuse to acknowledge that a stay-at-home mom is an equal financial partner in the marriage! **My wife of 30 years has always been a stay-at-home mom; I am proud of and indebted to her for the outstanding job she did raising our two children, now married.** Her job was made more challenging because of my many absences from home on overseas business trips. We title all properties in both our names. Examine your situation and get advice from a Christian perspective about your specific circumstances.

- As you consider the previous two bullets, I urge you to meditate on the significance of **Genesis 2:24:** "Therefore a man leaves his father and his mother and clings to his wife, and they become one flesh."

What does one flesh mean to you?

_____

_____

_____

_____

72. **What process or processes will you follow to decide on major purchases such as buying a house or a car?**

_____

_____

_____

_____

73. **What criteria do you use to decide between owning versus renting a home?**

_____

_____

_____

_____

74. **What happens if you can't agree on a common result? Do you do the following? Yes or no?**

74.1 Surrender all decisions to Christ? _____

74.2 Pray and seek to know God's will? _____

74.3 Strive for unanimity always? _____

74.4 Other, explain. _____

75. **As a couple, will you commit to starting and maintaining a capital fund from which you make all major purchases apart from monthly mortgage payments on your principal residence? How will you compute the capital fund?**

_____

_____

_____

_____

75.1 As a couple, what payments will you make from the **capital fund?**

_____
_____
_____
_____

76. **Will you aim to be debt-free and borrow to buy your principal residence only?**

_____
_____
_____
_____

77. **When do you start to save for your children's education expenses?**

77.1 **One year** before you need to start spending? _____

77.2 **Five years** before you need to start spending?_____

77.3 **In time** to accumulate the amount you will need when you need it?_____

77.4 **Never,** because you hope to have funds available when needed? _____

77.5 What factors should influence your final decision? _____

_____
_____
_____
_____

78. **What is your view of giving as a couple? Do you give based on your combined income? Remember that God owns it all and He loves a hilarious giver! (2 Corinthians 9:7).**

_____
_____
_____
_____
_____
_____
_____
_____
_____

Your first source for answers to principles to guide you should be the Bible. Additionally, I encourage you to get Christian pre-marital counselling that includes managing money.

As you begin the marriage, save 100% of the wife's income if you plan to start a family. Why the wife's income? Her income is the one that will be stopped if she takes time off to raise children. If you agree that the husband will be a stay-at-home dad to raise the kids, save 100% of his income, instead. The bottom line is this: Learn to live on one salary early if you plan for either husband or wife to stay home and raise the kids.

Even if you have been married for several years and one spouse will not stay at home, try to use one income only in the family budget while saving the other. It is never too late to try to live on one income and save the other. Certainly, it will be more difficult the longer you are married, but not impossible. Of course, I am suggesting that both incomes be pooled though allocated in this manner. I have seen couples who manage money as singles—each spending as he or she decides! This means neither partner has the full picture when making decisions. This approach encourages the my-money-your-money syndrome, which ignores the fact that it's God's money! Allocate the income to be saved to the **capital fund**. This is an excellent way to become and remain debt free.

79. **Rewrite Malachi 2:16 in your own words.**

_____

_____

_____

_____

To operate the **PEACE** system, one person should record spending, but both should develop the **plan** and **estimate** (the budget). Both should agree on an **upper limit** of spending, beyond which the **affordability index** applies. Both should participate in the **control phase** of the **PEACE** system (**Act**, **Compare**, and **Execute**), particularly the **executing** of changes to stay on course to achieve the **goals**.

Children

Money management principles for children and adults are identical. The key, therefore, is to let your children observe you controlling money. Be their example, so that their instinctive responses will be the "right way" they saw Mom and Dad functioning.

Teach your children to depend on Christ. Let them observe you doing so. I got a wake-up call about 19 years ago when Keisha (my daughter, then 10 years old) designed a special card titled "To: Father." Below this title, on the front, she drew Confucius. This was an excellent drawing in great detail. He was dressed in a blue robe, arms crossed in front, and he wore a traditional Chinese hat.

Keisha, Shabbir (my son), and Doreen (my wife) signed this card and presented it to me. It contained this quotation that they claimed was from (you guessed!) Confucius: **"The nobler man first practiceth what he preacheth and afterwards preacheth according to his practice."** Wow! What a powerful message! I got it then, and I am continually aware of it today. Yes, this is exactly what our Lord teaches us. I must ensure that I walk my talk! This card is hung in my study where I see it daily. I thank God for the openness and love of my family that led to this wake-up call!

At age six or seven, when they start to appreciate that **you need money** to buy things for them, give each of your children an allowance, no matter how small. Let them earn the allowance by doing a few small chores, so that they may develop a responsible attitude towards work. From this allowance teach them to give—including a tithe—to save, and to budget. Yes, to budget using the **PEACE** system, but keep it simple!

Teach them to set realistic goals and to work diligently to achieve these goals. It has been a joy to watch Bill and Keisha start our seven-year-old granddaughter Adrienne with an allowance from which she is tithing and saving! Presently, she is not as happy with tithing as with saving!

Never give your young children loans! Teach them to save for their purchases. Give them the keys to unlock their potential! Let them see Christ in you.

As your children mature, the chores should change along with the allowance. For a few years before Shabbir left home for university in British Columbia, he and I had a formal, written, annual snow removal contract (Doreen was his self-appointed lawyer). This included my responsibilities and his. I provided a snow blower in good working condition, and he had to ensure that our driveway was cleared completely before seven a.m. whenever it snowed. I paid him the going market rate, and he had to perform. The contract included a penalty clause for non-performance to an agreed standard and an incentive clause for performance beyond that standard. I am happy to report that I was never delayed because of his poor performance. Indeed, most years he earned a bonus.

Encourage your **teenage children** to develop goals and plans, and to allocate budgets for the following expense elements:

- **Giving**: They should develop an instinctive response to give at least 10% of all income received.
- **Saving**: Encourage them to save for specific purchases.
- **Capital Fund**: This is the basis for them to enter adulthood debt-free and to continue in that manner. **They should save 50% of all income.** Unlike the savings account, from which they may withdraw to purchase specific items, they should not use their **capital fund** except for large capital items such as a car, wedding expenses, university education expenses, down payment on a home, purchase and repairs of appliances, etc. Their **capital fund** is for the same purposes as yours, except they will start it early!
- **Clothing**: They should buy all their clothes from this budget.
- **Entertainment**: This item is essential. The main purpose is for them to value the cost of eating out, going to the movies, video rentals, etc. Eating out can become expensive even at fast-food restaurants!

Both Keisha and Shabbir managed budgets while at university/Bible college in their teens. Each studied in a different province from where we were living at the time. We developed budgets with them jointly and held them responsible to achieve them. Monthly, each sent us actual expenses compared with budgets, plus receipts for expenses, to receive reimbursement for amounts spent.

Finally, hold your children accountable for work "contracted" and achievement of goals. Teach them to develop spending habits that honour God. Let them make decisions where feasible and make mistakes in the process. Teach them to learn from these mistakes. This is tough. Nevertheless, allow them this freedom, but be prepared to rescue them from harm. Praise and encourage them along the way. Most important, let them know that you love them unconditionally, as Jesus loves each of us.

80. **Read Deuteronomy 6:4-9 and answer the following questions:**
80.1 How do you teach diligently your children the Word?

_____

_____

_____

_____

80.2 How do you "bind them as a sign on your hand" (NKJV—verse 8)?

_____

_____

_____

_____

80.3 How do they become "frontlets between your eyes" (NKJV—verse 8)?

_____

_____

_____

_____

80.4 Is there any aspect of your relationship with your children that you sense needs strengthening?

_____

_____

_____

_____

81. **Read Proverbs 22:6 and answer this question:**
81.1 In what ways are you training your child in the "way he should go" (NKJV)?

_____

_____

_____

_____

_____

_____

Personal Notes

8

Hear, O Israel: The LORD is our God, the LORD alone.
You shall love the LORD your God with all your heart, and with all your soul,
and with all your might. Keep these words that I am commanding you today
in your heart. Recite them to your children and talk about them when you are
at home and when you are away, when you rise. Bind them as a sign on your hand,
fix them as an emblem on your forehead, and write them
on the doorposts of your house and on your gates
(Deuteronomy 6:4-9 NRSV).

Worksheets

✱ ✱ ✱

Life Goal Planning Sheets (LGPS)
Life Goal Monitoring Sheets (LGMS)
Net Worth Form
PEACE Budget Computation Forms (PBCF)
PEACE Budget Worksheets
The Affordability Index

Life Goal Planning Sheet (LGPS)—Example

*Many are the plans in the mind of a man, but it is the purpose
of the Lord that will be established (Proverbs 19:21).*

Name: Lofty Bimmer   **Period: Jan 2000 to Dec 2005**

Goal (Ultimate Destination) * * * Early Retirement	Elaboration of Goal Statement of goal, including all prerequisites and sub goals. (Must Satisfy Three "Cs": Clear, Complete, Concise) *Retire early after paying off mortgage; after saving for kid's education; and after identifying a second career.*	
Control Items[1]	**Ultimate Goal of Control Item** (The Destination)[2]	**Current Period's Target** (Interim Checkpoint)[3]
Early Repayment of Mortgage	*Repay mortgage before age 50. At age 40 outstanding balance should not exceed $50,000. At age 45, outstanding balance should not exceed $20,000.*	*Accelerate monthly payment by $500. Pay 50% of all bonus or extra funds received towards mortgage.*
	Interim Target at Earlier Age / **Target Age for Repayment**	**Specific Targets for Current Year**
Education	*Total education cost to be saved by age 40.*	*Set aside at least $3000 annually*

Life Goal Monitoring Sheet (LGMS)—Example

Many are the plans in the mind of a man, but it is the purpose
of the Lord that will be established (Proverbs 19:21).

Name: Period:

COMPARISON OF ACTUAL PROGRESS TOWARDS ACHIEVING GOALS AGAINST PLANNED PROGRESS

Goal (Ultimate Destination) * * * Early Retirement	Elaboration of Goal Precise statement of goal, including all prerequisites. **(Must Satisfy Three "Cs": Clear, Complete, Concise)** *Retire early after paying off mortgage; after saving for kid's education; and after identifying a second career.*
Control Item[4] (From LGPS) Control Item Goal (From LGPS)	*Early Repayment of Mortgage* *Repay mortgage before age 50. At age 40 outstanding balance should not exceed $50,000. At age 45, outstanding balance should not exceed $20,000.*
Date of Review	Comparison of Progress Against Goal
31 December 1999	*Actual balance outstanding $55,000.* *$5,000 less than original goal.*
31 January 2000	*Mortgage payments are ahead of plan, but interest rates are increasing. Consider increasing rate of principal reduction in March 2000. Mortgage balance is still $5000 less than original. Mortgage renewal in March 2000.*

What is impossible with men is possible with God (Luke 18:27 NIV).

Life Goal Planning Sheet (LGPS)

Many are the plans in the mind of a man, but it is the purpose
of the Lord that will be established (Proverbs 19:21).

Name: Period:

Goal (Ultimate Destination)	**Elaboration of Goal** Statement of goal, including all prerequisites, and sub goals. **(Must Satisfy Three "Cs": Clear, Complete, Concise)**	
Control Items	**Ultimate Goal of Control Item** (The Destination)	**Current Period's Target** (Interim Checkpoint)

Life Goal Monitoring Sheet (LGMS)

*Many are the plans in the mind of a man, but it is the purpose
of the Lord that will be established (Proverbs 19:21).*

Name: Period:

COMPARISON OF ACTUAL PROGRESS TOWARDS ACHIEVING GOALS AGAINST PLANNED PROGRESS

Goal (Ultimate Destination)	Elaboration of Goal Precise Statement of Goal, including all prerequisites. **(Must Satisfy Three "Cs": Clear, Complete, Concise)**
Control Item (From LGPS) **Control Item Goal** (From LGPS)	
Date of Review	**Comparison of Progress Against Goal**

What is impossible with men is possible with God (Luke 18:27 NIV).

Net Worth ("Material Worth") Statement

As At _____

Things I "Own" (Assets) $

Cash _____
Investments _____
Personal Effects _____
Car _____
Furniture _____
House _____
Others _____

Total

Things I "Owe" (Liabilities) $

Family Loans _____
Car Loan _____
Credit Card Balance _____
Mortgage _____
Others _____

Total All Loans

My Equity (Net Worth) Total _____

Analysis of Amounts Owing to Lenders

Lender's Name	$ Owing	Interest %	Comments

Eternal Goal:

I want to know Christ and the power of his resurrection and the fellowship of sharing in his sufferings, becoming like him in his death (Philippians 3:10 NIV).

Material Goals:

1. Accumulate Down Payment on Home in 3 years
2. Balanced Budget Every Year
3. Vacation Overseas Next Year

Budget Categories	Frequency of Income/Expenses			Monthly Budget
	Weekly	Monthly	Yearly	
Salary		3150		3150
Less: Giving		(415)		(415)
Less: Taxes		(600)		(600)
Less: Savings		(185)		(185)
Less: Capital Fund		(150)		(150)
Net Salary		1800		1800

PEACE Budget Computation Form (PBCF): Expenses—Example

Budget Categories	Frequency of Income/Expenses			Monthly Budget (1800)
	Weekly	Monthly	Yearly	
Rent		500		500
Car Expenses				
Loan Repay		300		300
Gasoline	15 ◄	(x 4=)		► 60
Maintenance			360	
Groceries	100 ◄	(x 4=)		► 400
Entertainment & Recreation				
Meals	50			200
Video Rental	20			80
Movies	10			40
Telephone		50		50
Clothing			480 ◄	(÷ 12 =) 40
Gifts				
Birthdays			60	5
Christmas			120	10
Contingency	21			85
Total Expenses	216	850	1020	1800

PEACE Budget Computation Form (PBCF): Income

Eternal Goal:

I want to know Christ and the power of his resurrection and the fellowship of sharing in his sufferings, becoming like him in his death (Philippians 3:10 NIV).

Material Goals:

1.
2.
3.

Budget Categories	Frequency of Income/Expenses			Monthly Budget
	Weekly	Monthly	Yearly	
Salary				
Less: Giving				
Less: Taxes				
Less: Savings				
Less: Capital Fund				
Net Salary				

_____

_____

_____

_____

_____

_____

_____

PEACE Budget Computation Form (PBCF): Expenses

Budget Categories	Frequency of Income/Expenses			Monthly Budget
	Weekly	Monthly	Yearly	
Contingency				
Total Expenses				

Before spending, transfer **monthly budgeted amounts** from the **PBCF** above to the appropriate section of the **PEACE** Budget Worksheet ("**PBW**") **below**.

_____

_____

_____

_____

_____

_____

PEACE Budget Worksheet (PBW)—Example

Sept '98	Description	Total	Rent	Car Loan	Gasoline	Car Repairs	Groceries	Meals	Video	Movies	Telephone	Clothes	Birthdays	Christmas	Contingency
1	Allocation Sep	1800	500	300	60	30	400	200	80	40	50	40	5	10	85
	Rent	500	500												
4	Lunch	35						35							
	Balance Left	1265	0	300	60	30	400	165	80	40	50	40	5	10	85
7	Provigo Supermarket	179					179								
	Balance Left	1086	0	300	60	30	221	165	80	40	50	40	5	10	85
9	Cinema/Telephone	30								15	15				
	Balance Left	1056	0	300	60	30	221	165	80	25	35	40	5	10	85
11	Shell Gas Station	25			25										
	Balance Left	1031	0	300	35	30	221	165	80	25	35	40	5	10	85
13	Royal Bank	300		300											
	Balance Left	731	0	0	35	30	221	165	80	25	35	40	5	10	85
15	Dinner	75						75							
	Balance Left	656	0	0	35	30	221	90	80	25	35	40	5	10	85
17	Provigo	150					150								
	Balance Left	506	0	0	35	30	71	90	80	25	35	40	5	10	85
21	Shell	15			15										
	Balance Left	491	0	0	20	30	71	90	80	25	35	40	5	10	85
23	Video	30							30						
	Balance Left	461	0	0	20	30	71	90	50	25	35	40	5	10	85
23	Provigo	100					100								
	Balance Left	361	0	0	20	30	-29	90	50	25	35	40	5	10	85
27	Sears	76										76			
	Balance Left	285	0	0	20	30	-29	90	50	25	35	-36	5	10	85
29	Telephone	30									30				
30	Balance Left	255	0	0	20	30	-29	90	50	25	5	-36	5	10	85
30	Budget Oct 1998	1800	500	300	60	30	400	200	80	40	50	40	5	10	85
	Allocation Oct	2055	500	300	80	60	371	290	130	65	55	4	10	20	170

PEACE Budget Worksheet (PBW)

DATE:	Description	Total										
	Budget Month:											

PEACE Budget Worksheet (PBW)

DATE:	Description	Total											
	Budget Month:												

The Affordability Index

Spending Decisions						
Objective of Spending						
PLAN						
In or Can Be Accomodated	0	0	0	0	0	0
Out & Cannot Be Accomodated	2	2	2	2	2	2
LOANS						
Unchanged	0	0	0	0	0	0
Increase	6	6	6	6	6	6
ALTERNATIVE						
None	0	0	0	0	0	0
Yes	2	2	2	2	2	2
NECESSARY						
Yes	0	0	0	0	0	0
No	4	4	4	4	4	4
EFFECTIVE						
Yes	0	0	0	0	0	0
No	6	6	6	6	6	6
TOTAL of Highlighted Numbers						

The Affordability Index Scoring Regime

Scores	Results
< 6	You can afford the item
6 & above (except for a **vase** and a car)	You can't afford the item
8 or less	• You can afford the item as a **vase** • You may buy a car under specific conditions

Before spending any amount, whether by cash, cheque, or credit card, check the PBW for the available budget. After spending, enter the required details of the transaction on the PBW.

---

[1] A "Control Item" is a specific element of your life goal to be monitored. It is a stage of your journey toward your goal. A goal of a healthy lifestyle may have been jogging or weight loss as a control item.

[2] "Goal of Control Item" is the "destination" of the control item. For a "healthy lifestyle" it could be losing 30 pounds over six months.

[3] "Target for Period" could be "loss of five pounds monthly"; Sometimes "Goal" and "Target" are the same.

[4] Use one form per control item. For a goal of a healthy lifestyle, this form could track progress for the "loss of weight" control item.

About the Author

Michel A. Bell (Mike) has been married to Doreen Bell for over 30 years. They have four adult children, Bill Matheuszik (son-in-law), who is married to Keisha, and Shabbir, who is married to Lesley Ann (daughter-in-law), and three grandchildren, Adrienne, Jesse, and Dylan.

Michel and Doreen are Jamaican-born Canadians living in Baie d'Urfe, Quebec. The couple has lived in five countries, including Japan, the United Kingdom, and the USA.

Mike has held many senior finance positions in Montreal based Alcan Aluminum Limited, including Regional Vice President Finance and Legal for Alcan's Pacific subsidiary, and Chief Financial Officer for Alcan's world-wide Alumina and Chemicals businesses. Currently, Mike is Director of Business Planning for the world-wide Alumina and Chemicals group. He holds a master's degree in Management Science from the Sloan School of Management at Massachusetts Institute of Technology (M.I.T.), is a Chartered Certified Accountant (UK), and is the author of *Managing God's Money—The Basics*, published by Essence Publishing of Belleville, Ontario.

Encouraged by his children, ten years ago Mike began presenting basic money management concepts and principles to individuals, couples, and groups.

Order Form

To order additional copies of *Managing God's Money—The Basics* or *Managing God's Money—The Basics: Workbook*, please use the order form below.

Ordered By: (please print)

Name: _____

Address: _____

City: _____ Prov./State: _____

Postal/Zip Code: _____ Telephone: _____

Managing God's Money—The Basics   _____ copies @ $14.95 Cdn/$10.95 US: $_____

Managing God's Money—The Basics: **Workbook**   _____ copies @ $14.95 Cdn/$10.95 US: $_____

Shipping: ($3.00 first book – $1.00 each add. book) $_____

G.S.T. @ 7% (**Canadian Residents Only**): $_____

Total amount enclosed: $_____

Payable by   ❑ Check ❑ Money Order ❑ VISA or ❑ MasterCard

Credit Card #:_____ Expiry:_____

Signature:_____

Send to: Essence Publishing, 44 Moira Street West
Belleville, Ontario, Canada K8P 1S3

To order by phone, call our toll-free number,
1-800-238-6376
and have your credit card handy.